생활 속의 참선수행 Practice In Daily Life ⑦

한마음의 위력

The Infinite Power Of One Mind

한마음의 위력	
대행큰스님 법문	
생활 속의 참선수행 ⑦ / 한영합본	
발행일	2014년 1월 초판
	2014년 9월 재판
영문번역	한마음국제문화원
표지디자인	박수연
편집	한마음국제문화원
발행	한마음출판사
출판등록	384-2000-000010
전화	031-470-3175
팩스	031-470-3209
이메일	onemind@hanmaum.org

© 2014(재)한마음선원
본 출판물은 저작권법에 의하여 보호를 받는 저작물이므로 무단 복제와 무단 전재를 할 수 없습니다.

The Infinite Power Of One Mind
Dharma Talks by Seon Master Daehaeng
Practice in Daily Life ⑦
Bilingual Korean/English

First Edition Printed Jan. 2014
Second Edition Printed Sep. 2014
English Translation by
Hanmaum International Culture Institute
Edited by Hanmaum International Culture Institute
Cover Design by Su Yeon Park
Published by Hanmaum Publications

© 2014 Hanmaum Seonwon Foundation
All rights reserved, including the right to reproduce this work in any form.

Printed in the Republic of Korea

ISBN 978-89-91857-30-8 (04220)/978-89-951830-0-7(set)

국립중앙도서관 출판시도서목록(CIP)

한마음의 위력 = (The) infinite power of one mind : 대행큰스님 법문 / 영문번역 : 한마음국제문화원. -- [안양] : 한마음출판사, 2014
  p. ;   cm. -- (생활 속의 참선수행 = Practice in daily life ; 7)

한영 대역본임
ISBN 978-89-91857-30-8 04220 : ₩6000
ISBN 89-951830-0-7(세트) 04220

법문(불경)[法文]
224.2-KDC5
294.34-DDC21   CIP2013028523

The Infinite Power Of One Mind

Seon Master Daehaeng

한마음의 위력

대행큰스님 법문

세 번 죽어야 나를 보리라

우주 만유 크고 많으나
모두 한마음의 그림자라,
본래 공(空)한 자리에서 공한 것이 나오고
공해 사라지는 것이니,
나와 함께 들이고 내는 것 전부가
공함을 알면
한 번 죽음이라.

삼세의 부처님, 조사님과 선지식에서부터
풀 한 포기에 이르기까지,
일체 만물만생을 버리지 않고
공한 나와 함께 더불어 죽었으니
그대로가 진리임을 안다면
두 번 죽음이라.

Die Three Times and Truly See Yourself

Vast beyond imagining
filled with an infinite variety of life,
yet everything in this universe
is but a shadow of one mind.
From an inherently empty place
appear empty things.
Being empty,
they all vanish.
If I truly realize that everything I interact with is empty,
this is dying one time.

From great Buddhas who rule the heavenly realms,
to tiny weeds alongside the road,
die together with them all
without excluding a single one,
die together with this empty "me,"
and realize that everything, just as it is,
is the truth.
This is dying a second time.

일체 만물 유정 무정 나 아님 없으니
너와 나 우리 모두 한자리 한몸이다.
일체 만유 모두가 자불自佛의 나툼이니,
유생 무생 자재自在면
세 번 죽음이라.

일체 만법 들이고 내는
내 한마음이 주인공主人空이니
죽어야 살리라.
세 번 죽어야 나를 보리라.

-대행큰스님 게송-

Among all the people, plants, and animals,
among the stones and the clouds,
there is nothing that is not me.
You and I,
all of us together,
are sharing the same place
and the same body.
Everything is the manifestation of this inherent Buddha,
so when can you freely take care of everything with life,
and without life,
this is called dying a third time.

Your one mind, which brings in and sends out everything
is your true foundation, that which does things.
We have to die in order to truly live,
die three times and see yourself.

— Daehaeng Kun Sunim —

차 례

12 머리글

16 대행큰스님에 대하여

24 한마음의 위력

Contents

13 Foreword

17 About Daehaeng Kun Sunim

25 The Infinite Power of One Mind

머리글

대행큰스님께서 지난 50여 년 동안 끊임없이 중생들에게 베풀어주신 수많은 법문이 있었지만, 핵심을 짚어내는 단 하나의 단어가 있다면, 그건 아마도 "참나"일 것입니다. 항상 나와 함께 있어서 보지 못하는 내 안의 진짜 나, 그 "참나"를 발견하여 당당하고 싱그럽게 살아가기를 바라는, 중생을 위한 스님의 간절한 바램은 이 한 편의 법문 속에도 여지없이 드러나 있습니다.

누구에게나 내면에는 만물만생을 다 먹여 살리고도 되남는 마음 속 한 점의 불씨가 있습니다. 그 영원한 불씨를 찾아 광대무변한 마음법의 이치를 체득하여, 진정한 자유인으로서, 우주의 한 일원으로서 당당히 그 역할을 해나가길 바라는 대행큰스님의 간곡한 뜻이 이 법문을 통해 여러분 모두의 마음에 전해지길 바랍니다.

한마음국제문화원 일동 합장

Foreword

Over the last fifty years, Daehaeng Kun Sunim has given countless Dharma talks and teachings to beings without number, but if all those talks could be summed up into one word, it would be "true self."

This true essence has always been with us, yet remains unseen. Discover it for yourself, and in doing so, learn to live with courage, dignity, and joy. That all beings should awaken to this true essence is Daehaeng Kun Sunim's deepest wish. When you've tasted the purest, most refreshing spring water imaginable, you naturally want to share it with others.

Within us all is this seed, this spark that feeds and sustains each and every being. Discover this eternal spark and realize its profound and unlimited ability. If you can do this, you'll know what it means to truly be a free person, and you can fulfill the great role that is yours as a member of the whole universe.

With palms together,
The Hanmaum International Culture Institute

 사랑하는 큰스님

살아생전 우리에게 보여주신 그 마음, 그 가르침
놓지 않고 가겠습니다
대장부가 되겠습니다.

당신을 만날 수 있어 감사했습니다.

Dear Kun Sunim,

How can words possibly express our gratitude
for how much your wisdom and compassion
have meant to us?
We'll take what you've taught us and put it
into practice throughout our daily lives.
Sharing it with all we meet,
we'll strive to become a light
to everyone around us.

Having you in our lives has been such a blessing.

대행큰스님에 대하여

대행큰스님은 여러 면에서 매우 보기 드문 선사(禪師)셨다. 무엇보다 선사라면 당연히 비구 스님을 떠올리는 전통 속에서 여성으로서 선사가 되었으며, 비구 스님들을 제자로 두었던 유일한 비구니 스님이었고, 노년층 여성이 주된 신도계층을 이루었던 한국 불교에 젊은 세대의 청장년층 남녀들을 대거 참여하게 만들어 한국불교에 새로운 풍격(風格)을 일으키는데 일조한 큰 스승이셨다. 또한 어느 누구나 마음수행을 통해 깨달을 수 있음을 강조하며 전통적인 수행 모델과는 달리 삭발제자와 유발제자를 가리지 않고 법을 구하는 이들에게는 모두 똑같이 가르침을 주셨고, 전통 비구니 강원과 비구니 종단에 대한 지속적인 지원을 펼치심으로써 비구니 승단을 발전시키는데 중추적인 역할을 하셨다.

About Daehaeng Kun Sunim

Daehaeng *Kun Sunim*[1] (1927-2012) was a rare teacher in Korea: a female *Seon(Zen)*[2] master, a nun whose students included monks as well as nuns, and a teacher who helped revitalize Korean Buddhism by dramatically increasing the participation of young people and men. She broke out of traditional models of spiritual practice to teach in such a way that allowed anyone to practice and awaken, making laypeople a particular focus of her efforts. At the same time, she was a major force for the advancement of *Bhikkunis*,[3] heavily supporting traditional nuns' colleges as well as the modern Bhikkuni Council of Korea.

---

1. Sunim / Kun Sunim: Sunim is the respectful title of address for a Buddhist monk or nun in Korea, and Kun Sunim is the title given to outstanding nuns or monks.

2. Seon (Chan, Zen): Seon describes the unshakeable state where one has firm faith in their inherent foundation, their Buddha-nature, and so returns everything they encounter back to this fundamental mind. It also means letting go of "I," "me," and "mine" throughout one's daily life.

3. Bhikkunis: Female sunims who are fully ordained are called Bhikkuni(比丘尼), while male sunims who are fully ordained are called Bhikku(比丘). This can also be a polite way of indicating male or female sunims.

대행스님은 1927년 서울에서 태어나 일찍이 9세경에 자성을 밝히시고, 일제 강점기와 6.25 전쟁을 거치면서 당신이 증득(證得)하신 바를 완성하기 위해 오랫동안 산중에서 수행하셨다. 1950년대 말경, 치악산 상원사 근처에 있는 한 움막에 머무르시며 찾아오는 수많은 사람들의 고통스런 호소를 들으시고 그들을 도와주셨다. 중생들이 가지고 오는 어떠한 문제도, 어떠한 어려운 상황도 해결이 되도록 도와주신 대행스님의 자비의 원력은 당시에 이미 한국에서는 전설이 되어 있었다. 스님은 자비를 물 마른 웅덩이에서 죽어가는 물고기를 살리는 방생에 비유하셨다. 그래서 집세가 없어 셋집에서 쫓겨난 사람들에게 집을 마련해 주고, 학비가 없어서 학교를 마칠 수 없는 학생들에게 학비를 대주셨지만, 스님의 자비행(慈悲行)을 아는 사람은 거의 없을 정도였다.

그러나, 문제를 해결해 주면 그때뿐 또 다른 문제가 닥쳐오면 속수무책이 되어 버리고 마는 사람들을 보며, 스님께서는 중생들이 자신들의 문제를 스스로 해결하고, 나아가 인과(因果)와 윤회(輪廻)[1]의 굴레에서 벗어나 자유인이 될 수 있는 도리를 가르치는 것이 더 시급하다는 생각을 하게 되셨다.

Born in Seoul, Korea, she awakened when she was around eight years old and spent the years that followed learning to put her understanding into practice. For years, she wandered the mountains of Korea, wearing ragged clothes and eating only what was at hand. Later, she explained that she hadn't been pursuing some type of asceticism; rather, she was just completely absorbed in entrusting everything to her fundamental *Buddha*[4] essence and observing how that affected her life.

Those years profoundly shaped Kun Sunim's later teaching style; she intimately knew the great potential, energy, and wisdom inherent within each of us, and recognized that most of the people she encountered suffered because they didn't realize this about themselves. Seeing clearly the great light in every individual, she taught people to rely upon this inherent foundation, and refused to teach anything that distracted from this most important truth.

Her deep compassion made her a legend in Korea long before she formally started teaching.

---

4. Buddha: In this text, "Buddha" and "Bodhisattva" are capitalized out of respect, because these represent the essence and function of the enlightened mind. "The Buddha" always refers to Shakyamuni Buddha.

마침내 산에서 내려온 스님께서는 1972년 경기도 안양에 한마음선원을 설립하셨고, 이후 40여 년 동안 한마음선원에 주석하시며, 크고 작은 법회에서 질문을 해오는 사람들에게 그들의 근기와 여건에 맞추어 답을 해주시며 불법의 진리를 가르쳐 주셨다. 스님은 여러 다양한 사회복지 프로그램을 후원하셨고, 6개국에 10개의 해외지원과 한국 국내에 15개 지원을 세우셨으며, 스님의 가르침은 영어, 독어, 스페인어, 러시아어, 중국어, 일본어, 불어, 이태리어, 베트남어, 인도네시아어, 아랍어 등으로 번역 출간되었다. 2012년 5월 22일 영시, 세납 86세로 입적하셨으며, 법랍 63세 이셨다.

---

1. **윤회**(輪廻): 산스크리트의 삼사라(samsara)를 번역한 말로 쉼 없이 돈다는 생사의 바퀴를 뜻함. 다시 말해, 수레바퀴가 끊임없이 구르는 것과 같이, 중생이 번뇌와 업에 의하여 삼계(三界: 색계, 욕계, 무색계) 육도(六道: 지옥, 아귀, 축생, 아수라, 인간, 천상)라는 생사의 세계를 그치지 않고 돌고 도는 현상을 일컬음.

She was known for having the spiritual power to help people in all circumstances with every kind of problem. She compared compassion to freeing a fish from a drying puddle, putting a homeless family into a home, or providing the school fees that would allow a student to finish high school. And when she did things like this, and much more, few knew that she was behind it.

Kun Sunim saw that for people to live freely and go forward in the world as a blessing to all around them, they needed to know about this bright essence that is within each of us. To help people discover this for themselves, she founded the first *Hanmaum*[5] Seon Center in 1972. For the next forty years she gave wisdom to those who needed wisdom, food and money to those who were poor and hungry, and compassion to those who were hurting.

---

5. Hanmaum[han-ma-um]: "Han" means one, great, and combined, while "maum" means mind, as well as heart, and together they mean everything combined and connected as one. What is called "Hanmaum" is intangible, unseen, and transcends time and space. It has no beginning or end, and is sometimes called our fundamental mind. It also means the mind of all beings and everything in the universe connected and working together as one. In English, we usually translate this as "one mind."

본 저서는 대행큰스님의 법문을
한국어와 영어 합본 시리즈로 출간하는
<생활 속의 참선수행> 시리즈 제7권으로써
1986년 4월 20일 정기 법회 때 설하신 내용을
재편집한 것입니다.

This Dharma talk was given by
Daehaeng Kun Sunim on Sunday, April 20, 1986.
This is Volume 7 in the ongoing series,
Practice in Daily Life.

Daehaeng Kun Sunim founded ten overseas branches of Hanmaum Seon Center, and her teachings have been translated into twelve different languages to date: English, German, Russian, Chinese, French, Spanish, Indonesian, Italian, Japanese, Vietnamese, Estonian, and Arabic, in addition to the original Korean. For more information about these or the overseas centers, please see the back of this book for details.

한마음[2]의 위력

1986년 4월 20일

　마음을 차분하게 가라앉히고 잘 들으세요. 차분하지 못하다면 바로 들어가지를 못합니다. 지금 불법의 교리를 그냥 그냥 얘기하는 게 아닙니다. 누구나가 공부하는 사람이라면 진짜 자기 주인공(主人空)[3]을 믿고 물러서지 않고, 항상 그 자리에다 일체를 맡겨, 근본을 통해 만법이 들고 나게 해야 합니다. 그리고 그렇게 해서 나오는 것까지도 놓고 맡기는 것을 반복해야 합니다. 그것이 참선이며 행선(行禪)입니다.

---

2. 한마음: '한'이란 광대무변함, 일체가 하나로 합쳐진 것을 뜻하며, 한마음이란 만질 수도 없고 보이지도 않으며, 시공간을 초월하고, 시작도 끝도 없는 근본마음을 말함. 또한, 만물만생의 마음이 삼천대천세계와 서로 연결되어 하나로 돌아가는 것을 의미하기도 함. 다시 말해, 한마음은 일체만물의 근본마음과 그 마음들이 하나로 돌아가는 작용을 모두 다 포함하고 있음.

3. 주인공(主人空): 우리 모두 스스로 갖추어 가지고 있는 근본마음으로 일체 만물만생의 근본과 직결된 자리. 나를 존재하게 하고, 나를 움직이게 하고, 내 모든 것을 관장하는 참 주인이므로 주인(主人)이며, 매 순간 쉴 사이 없이 변하고 돌아가 고정된 실체가 없으므로 비어 있다고 할 수 있기 때문에 빌 공(空)자를 써서, 주인공(主人空)이라 함. 본래면목, 성품, 불성 등 여러 가지로 지칭할 수 있음.

The Infinite Power of One Mind

April 20, 1986

Deeply settle your minds and listen carefully. If you're not calm, if you're not settled down, you can't take the direct route [pointing to her chest].

What we're talking about today isn't just theory or philosophy. If you're serious about spiritual practice, then you need to have steady faith in your true nature, *Juingong.*[6] You must always entrust everything to that place, and go forward relying upon this foundation in everything you do. After entrusting, take what comes out and entrust that to your foundation as well. Again and again, you have to keep returning everything to your foundation. This is

---

6. Juingong (主人空): Pronounced "ju-in-gong." Juin (主人) means the true doer or the master, and gong (空) means "empty." Thus Juingong is our true nature, our true essence, the master within that is always changing and manifesting, without a fixed form or shape.

Daehaeng Sunim has compared Juingong to the root of the tree. Our bodies and consciousness are like the branches and leaves, but it is the root that is the source of the tree, and it is the root that sustains the visible tree.

왜 내가 이런 말을 항상 되풀이하고 넘어가느냐 하면은, 여러분이 그렇게 안 하신다면 앞으로 본인에게도 이득이 하나도 없고 또 지구라는 배 안에서 사는 다른 생명들에게도 이익이 하나도 없기 때문입니다.

모든 무정물이나 식물이나 동물들에 이름을 지어 부르고 그것을 배웁니다. 그리고 그걸 기본으로 과학이니 철학이니 생물학이니 또는 정치니 공학이니 하는 분야들이 점차적으로 나왔습니다. 문학도 그렇고 의학도 그렇고 말입니다. 그런데 이렇게 분류를 해가며 이름을 짓고 체계화시켜 가다 보니 이론적인 학문이 발전돼 유식하게는 됐지만 우리가 실천으로 옮기지 못하고 그 본질을 놓치는 바람에 우리의 정신이 계발되지 못해 바로 지난 세월 우리가 많은 어려움을 겪었습니다.

그러나 우리가 앞으로 인간으로서의 주어진 능력으로 행(行)을 해나갈 수 있다면 그대로 우리 역사가 달라지며 차원이 달라질 겁니다. 그러므로 우리가 지금 말하고 있는 이것이 '말로 떨어지는 말'이 아니라 법이 될 수 있게끔, 생활에 실천으로 보급이 될 수 있는 그런 법도가 이루어져야 됩니

the meaning of meditation, and is meditation in action. Do you know why I keep bringing this up whenever we meet? Because if you do otherwise, nothing you do will truly benefit yourself, nor will it have any benefit for the other beings living with us on this ship we call the Earth.

As we humans have examined the world around us, we've given names to all the plants, animals, and inanimate objects. From this activity, diverse fields of study have gradually arisen, such as biology, philosophy, engineering, literature, politics, and medicine. Even hundreds of years ago, this process had generated a huge amount of theoretical knowledge about the world and how we should live. However, it wasn't put into practice, and so people lost sight of what is very fundamental to us. Because of this, we have been slow to develop the spiritual side of things, and people have suffered terribly over the centuries.

If we can just use the abilities inherent within every human being, our future and the level of our existence will change. So take what we're talking about and apply it to all the things that arise in your daily life. By doing this, the energy of your practice will spread to others, and your words and actions will become manifestations

다. 나는 이렇게 생각합니다. 지금 말하는 이 말 자체가 현재의 삶 속에서 실제로, 일체 만물 유생(有生) 무생(無生)에서 다 같이 이루어져 우주의 개발과 우리 인간의 계발이 동시에 실천에 옮겨져야 된다는 얘깁니다.

여러분은 항상 눈에 보이는 것만 생각하시는데 그런 것들은 한 찰나에 눈에 보였다가도 모습이 바뀌어지면 알아보지 못합니다. 모습만 이 모습이 되고 저 모습이 되고 그러는데, 찰나찰나에 돌아가는 그 자체를 모르기 때문에 '죽는다, 산다'는 소리가 나오는 겁니다. 만물만생은 본래 죽고 사는 게 없으며 바로 모습만 바뀌어 옮겨 놓여질 뿐이지 죽는 게 없습니다. 본래 나고 죽는 게 없다는 뜻입니다. 따라서 생사윤회도 업보도 인과도 모두가 여러분의 **한생각**[4]에 달려 있습니다. 그런데 그것마저도 없다고 하는 이유는 너무 찰나찰나 돌아가기 때문에 인과응보나 유전성이나 윤회가 붙을 사이가 없기에 그런 겁니다.

---

4. 한생각: 어떤 생각을 우리들 내면의 근본자리에 입력시키거나 맡겨놓았을 때, 근본을 통해 나오는 생각은 우리들 몸속의 모든 생명들뿐만 아니라 이 세상의 만물만생에 전달되며, 일체가 그 생각에 응하게 됨. 보이지 않는 정신계, 즉 우리들 근본마음을 통해 일으켜지는 생각은 물질계에서 현실로 나타나게 됨. 이렇게 근본을 통해 나오게 되는 생각을 한생각이라 함.

of the Dharma. Further, in addition to applying this practice to your daily life, you have to apply it to all beings, both living and dead, as well as to the inanimate world. You must apply your practice toward developing the universe as well as yourself.

People tend to believe only in what they can see with their eyes, so when something abruptly changes, they no longer recognize it. Both people and things take on one shape, and then put on another shape, and still yet another. People talk about things like "living" and "dying" because they don't know the reality: that it is all changing, every single instant. Inherently, there is no living or dying, because everything is only changing its shape and moving from here to there. Thus, ultimately, birth, death, karma, cause and effect, and rebirth all happen according to the thoughts you give rise to. Sometimes it's even said that these things don't exist, because everything is changing every instant. Nothing remains behind for birth and death, cause and effect, and even karma and genetics to stick to.

I learned this long ago when I lived in the mountains. One day after an icy snow covered the mountains, I found that the road I was on

그 뜻을 제가 안 것은 아주 예전입니다. 산에 있을 때 하루는 눈이 와서 사람이 발을 딛지 못하리만큼 아주 미끄러웠습니다. 유리알처럼 미끄럽고 아주 가파랐죠. 그런데 거기를 지나가려니까 양쪽으로는 디딜 데가 없고 외길인데다 유리알 같으니 어떻게 발을 붙이면서 가겠습니까? 그래 거길 미끄러지듯 내리뛰었습니다. 만약에 발을 떼어놓을 때에 머뭇머뭇하면서 붙어 서 있었더라면 제대로 가기는커녕 바로 서 있지도 못했을 겁니다. 그러니 멈추지 말고 발을 떼어 놓아야 했습니다. 우리의 삶이 이와 같습니다. 잠시라도 고정되어 멈춰서 있게 되면 찰나찰나 쉬지 않고 돌아가고 있는 이 세상 진리에 상응하며 함께 흘러갈 수 없다 이겁니다.

여기에서 납득한 게 뭐냐 하면, 우리가 찰나찰나 옮겨놓고 옮겨가고 하면서 모습을 바꿔놓는 진화력이나 창조력 또는 **타심력**(他心力), **숙명력**(宿命力), **천이력**(天耳力), **천안력**(天眼力), **신족력**(神足力)[5]을 포함한 모든 능력이 우리들한테 주어져 있

---

5. 오신통(五神通): 불교의 육신통(六神通) 중에서 누진통(漏盡通)을 뺀 다섯 가지의 신통(능력), 즉 천안통(天眼通), 천이통(天耳通), 타심통(他心通), 숙명통(宿命通), 신족통(神足通)을 일컬음. 천안통(天眼通)은 보는 사이 없이 볼 수 있는 능력, 천이통(天耳通)은 듣는 사이 없이 들을 수 있는 능력, 타심통(他心通)은 다른 이의 마음을 아는 사이 없이 알 수 있는 능력, 숙명통(宿命通)은 과거 어디로부터 왔는지를 아는 사이 없이 아는 능력, 신족통(神足通)은 한 찰나에 가고 옴이 없이 가고 올 수 있는 능력을 말함.

had become very slippery. What's more, it was heading downhill and becoming very steep. It was like walking on glass, but I found that if I took very short, fast steps, I could work my way down it. However, if I hesitated and stood still for even a moment, I would immediately begin to slide sideways, and would fall down. I had to keep my feet moving; they couldn't remain motionless. Our lives are just like this: we have to be able to move with the ever-changing nature of the world.

Later, as I reflected upon this experience, I suddenly realized that we have within each of us all of the powers of evolution and creation, which makes it possible for us to be constantly moving and changing, and to even change our shapes. Likewise, we are also endowed with the five subtle powers. These are the ability to see everything everywhere, the ability to hear everything, to travel without moving one's body, to know past lives, and to know others' thoughts. For example, the ability to hear everything can also be called the power of communication. However, these days, we use phones and radios. Likewise, people use telescopes to substitute for our inherent ability to see everything in the universe. We are all endowed with these kinds of abilities, but we are

다는 것입니다. 예를 들어, 천이력이라고 하는 것은 통신력이라 할 수 있는데 오늘날의 통신기기나 레이더 같은 걸 만들어 대처하고 있고, 천안력이라는 것도 천체망원경 같은 기기를 만들어 대처하고 있지요. 우리에게 이렇듯 능력이 갖춰져 있는데도 우리는 주어진 그 능력을 제대로 활용하지 못하고 있습니다. 그럼 50%가 모자란다고 볼 수밖엔 없죠. 하지만 우리가 세상 돌아가는 이치, 이 마음도리를 알면 50%가 채워져서 100%의 제대로 된 행을 할 수가 있다는 얘깁니다. 그렇게 될 수만 있다면 이것은 죽은 불교가 아니라 생동력 있게 살아나갈 수 있고 삶의 보람을 느낄 수 있는 산 불교가 되겠죠. 봄이 되면 저렇게 진달래가 피고 개나리가 피고 목련이 피고, 온갖 꽃이 다 피고 온갖 풀이 다 파랗게 나고, 얼음이 녹아서 시냇물이 흐르고 새들이 울고 이러는데 이러한 것이 **불국토**(佛國土)[6]와 무엇이 다르겠습니까?

---

6. 불국토(佛國土): 일반적으로 부처님이 계시는 국토 혹은 부처님이 교화하는 국토를 이르는 것으로 원래 극락(極樂)등의 정토(淨土)를 가르키는 것이었으나, 후에는 예토(穢土) 또한 부처님이 교화하는 곳이므로 불국토로 이해하게 됨. 여기서는 물질적으로나 정신적으로 걸림없이 평화롭게 삶을 살아갈 수 있는 세상을 지칭함.

unable to properly use them. It can honestly be said that we are missing fifty percent of ourselves.

However, if we understand the principles of how the world works — the principles of our fundamental *mind*[7] — then the missing fifty percent is filled in, and we are able to properly use all one hundred percent. This is living Buddhism, which fills people with energy and awakens them to the worth of life. When spring comes, everything comes alive and blossoms naturally. The azaleas, forsythias, and magnolias all send forth flowers; every kind of plant turns green, the frozen ice melts, and the valleys fill with bubbling streams and singing birds. The Buddha's Pure Land is also attained like this.

If we understand this principle and can continuously apply it as we go through life, it becomes a great tool for us. It's as if we have our own magic wand. With a wave of it, everything becomes possible. This place where everything becomes one — one mind — is the essence of the Earth, of the sun, and of the very universe itself.

---

7. Mind(心)(Kor. –maum): In Mahayana Buddhism, "mind" refers to this fundamental mind, and almost never means the brain or intellect. It is intangible, beyond space and time, and has no beginning or end. It is the source of everything, and everyone is endowed with it.

우리가 그 도리를 알아서 앞으로 해나갈 수 있는 지혜가 바로 찰나찰나 무기가 된다면, 그 하나가 바로 '은 나와라 뚝딱! 금 나와라 뚝딱!'하는 옛날 이야기처럼 최고의 도깨비방망이가 될 수 있겠죠. 한마음의 한 점은 바로 우주의 근본이며, 태양의 근본이며, 바로 천지의 근본이 될 수 있기에 그렇게 위대하다는 겁니다. 그 위대한 한 점이 바로 '은 나와라 뚝딱, 금 나와라 뚝딱'인데, 그렇게 해서 나오는 보배만을 말하는 게 아니라 나오는 것도, 주는 것도, 하는 것도, 드는 것도, 덮는 것도, 굴리는 것도 모두 그 한 점의 마음에 있다는 얘깁니다.

그리고 여러분이 공부를 해서 그 한 점의 마음을 잘 요리할 수 있다면, 다시 말해, 지금 우리 마음 자체를 바깥으로 굴리지 않고 안으로 잘 굴린다면, 안으로 굴린 거기서 자연스럽게 나오는 한 생각에 우주 개발도 할 수 있는 능력이 담기게 되는 겁니다. 그렇게 되면 우주 개발이 곧 우리가 살아나가는 생활 속에 있게 되는 것이니 그게 바로 신성한 우주 개발이란 얘기죠. 내가 우주 개발 얘기하니까 그러면 '우주만 중요하고 여기는 아니냐?' 그럴 수 있는데 그런 게 아닙니다. 모두가 신성한 곳입니다.

It's so incredible! This magnificent one place, this one single point, produces everything. It's where everything is connected. It can give, do, support, embrace, and turn things around. Your own fundamental mind can do all of this!

So take this one place, this one mind, and try to skillfully apply it to everything. By "skillfully," I mean returning your thoughts and feelings inwardly, as opposed to directing them outwardly. If you return all of these things inwardly, *"one thought"*[8] will naturally arise from there, and within that "one thought" is the power to change and develop even the universe. If you can practice like this, the entire universe exists right there, in your daily life, and as you take care of your daily life, you also take care of the universe. How could this work be anything other than sacred?!

I hope that you will listen carefully to what I'm saying, and won't dismiss it as just some lecture. What I'm talking about are the things that

---

8. One Thought: This refers to the ability to raise and then input and entrust a thought to our foundation. When we can connect with our foundation like this, then through our foundation, that thought spreads to everything in the universe, including all of the lives in our body. At that instant, because all things are fundamentally not two, they all respond to that thought.

내 말을 단지 설법으로만 듣고 그냥 귓전으로 흘려버리지 않았으면 좋겠습니다. 나는 지금 우리 생활에서 벌어지고 있는 일, 우리가 해야만 하는 일에 대해서 말하고 있는 것입니다. 사람들을 가르친답시고 듣기 좋은 말을 머리로 추려가지고 얘기하는 것이 아닙니다. 그런 것은 이미 죽은 설법입니다. 우리가 목마를 때 얼른 그냥 마시는 물이 내가 진짜 필요로 하는 유용한 물인 것처럼, 우리 앞에 닥친 문제들을 실질적으로 어떻게 그때그때 생활 속에서 해결할 수 있는지에 대한 이야기를 하는 것입니다.

나는 지금 국내외에서 벌어지는 일들, 혼돈이 일어나는가 하면 잔잔히 가라앉고, 가라앉는가 하면 일어나고 하는 그런 문제 등등을 풀기 어려운 문젯거리로 보지는 않습니다. 우주의 한마음 그 뜻이, 우리 지구를 지속시키는 반면에 모든 공해가 빠져 나가게 할 것입니다. 일련의 과정은 한마음 한뜻으로 조화를 이루며 굴곡이 지지 않고 평화스럽게 갈 수 있는 그런 기초를 닦기 위한 발판을 세우는 거라고 봅니다.

happen to us every day, and what we have to do to truly solve those. If I tried to give you clever or easy-to-follow Dharma talks, they would just be dead words. They would have no power to help you. When you're thirsty, you need water that you can drink right away. So, I'm trying to give you teachings that are useful and adaptable to your daily life, teachings that will help you grow and go forward.

From time to time, problems will occur in some country, or around the world, where an event throws everything into chaos. To me, those kinds of problems aren't difficult to solve. The will of one mind, which combines all the minds of the entire universe, works to sustain the Earth. It even causes all kinds of negative energies to dissipate. All of the ups and downs we go through as we practice are the preliminary steps that will eventually enable us to go forward peacefully and harmoniously, as one mind. Using what you've learned, you can help even the universe develop.

As I said earlier, when something changes, when it is moved from here to there, people have no idea what happened. It's like not noticing that the larva became a cicada, or that the cicada becomes the larva. Likewise, most people are unaware

그렇다면 국가적으로나, 세계적으로나, 우주적으로나 어떻게 해야 그런 거를 다 실천해서 평온을 가져올 수 있으며 이것이 우주의 개발이 될 수 있을까 하는 겁니다. 아까도 얘기했듯이 저기서 여기 옮겨 놓으면 모르고 여기서 저기 옮겨 놓으면 모릅니다. 굼벵이가 매미가 될 때 모르고 매미가 굼벵이가 될 때 모르듯이, 우리 인간도 그렇게 연쇄적으로 진화되면서 형성해 온 것을 모르고 돌아가고 있습니다.

그래도 우리가 많이 계발된 것이, 지금 유전자(genome, 유전체를 지칭)를 알게 됨으로써, 많은 물질이 바뀌어지기도 하고 또는 많이 나기도 하는 것을 연구해 낸 것입니다. 그런데 내가 생각할 때는 무루(無漏)의 무전자[7]로 하여금 유전자(여기

---

7. 무전자: 무(無)의 세계와 유(有)의 세계가 어울려 돌아갈 수 있게 해주는 매개체이다. 물질계에서 유전자들이 형성해 놓은 것들을 무의 세계와 균형 있게 돌아갈 수 있게 해주는 받침 역할을 한다. 달리 표현하자면, 정신계에서 물질계로의 오고 감이 자유로울 수 있도록 해주는, 그 어떤 것이라고 할 수 있다. 체(體)를 가지고 있는 상태에서는 이러한 역할을 할 수 없으므로, 체가 없다는 측면에서는 무의 세계에 속한다고 할 수도 있겠으나, 이것이 오고 가며 작용하여 보여지는 곳은 현상계이니, '무의 세계에 속한다, 유의 세계에 속한다'라고 구분 지어 말할 수는 없다. 한편, 여기서 유전자란, 의학에서 사용하는 용어, 'genome'이 아닌, 현상계(물질계)를 형성하고 돌아가게 하는 어떤 구성체를 뜻한다. 도저히 체를 가지고 있다고 할 수 없을 정도로 작아 모양을 규정지을 수는 없으나, 가느다란 형태, 또는, 그와 같은 움직임을 가지고 있다고 보여진다. 〈대행큰스님의 무전자와 유전자에 관한 설명 축약〉

that we human beings, too, have been constantly moving from one form to another and evolving.

Nonetheless, we've managed to develop quite a bit by relying upon things like genetics, and, by using this knowledge, to change plants and animals to increase production. But if we examine this at a deeper level, matter itself exists because of the unseen aspects of the non-material realms. From this arose what scientists call our genome, as well as all material things. Thus, this unseen aspect, what I sometimes call the *mujeonja*,[9] can cause DNA and genes

---

9. Mujeonja [/mu-jun-ja/]: The essence, or medium, that connects the material and non-material realms and allows them to function together harmoniously. It is the underlying essence that allows the balanced functioning of the non-material realm and what is manifested into the material realm. To put it another way, we call it something that allows the spiritual realms to freely interact with the material realm. If it had a physical essence, it couldn't perform this role, so it could be said that it belongs to the non-material realm. However, it is within the physical realm that the functioning of the mujeonja manifests, so we cannot say that it belongs to one realm or the other.

When the mujeonja manifests into the material realm, it works through a phenomena called "yujeonja"[/yu-jun-ja/]. Its movement gives the appearance of infinitely tiny threads, but it is so small that it's impossible to detect any mass. It's this yujeonja that gives rise to everything in our physical world, and makes it possible for everything to function and interact.

서는 genome이 아님)가 있고 그로 인해 요새 과학에서 애기하는 유전자(genome, 유전체)도 생기고 물질도 나온다고 봅니다. 그렇다면은 무루의 무전자가 그 유전자(genome, 유전체)를 없앨 수도 있고 또 많이 생기게 할 수도 있는데, 그것은 바로 무전자의 원자력 때문이기도 하고 통신력 때문이기도 합니다. 그전에도 애기했듯이 하나가 되어 작용할 때, 거기에 붙으면 붙는 대로 소멸시키고 생성시키는 능력이 아주 광대무변하기 때문에 뭐든지 집어삼킬 수 있고, 그것을 요리해서 에너지로 만들고 영양소로 만들어서 여러분한테 이익도 줄 수 있는 그런 자유권이 있다는 애깁니다.

그럼으로써 이 지구에 있는 여러분이, 살아나가는 데 차원을 높여서 지금 현실에 적용해 살아나간다면 세계적으로 그 생활이나 모습이 달라질 겁니다. 역사가 달라질 겁니다. 예를 들어 지금은 여러분이 통신을 하거나 에너지를 사용할 때 여러 기계장치를 사용해야 가능하지만 한생각 내면 그냥 통과가 될 수 있는 그런 세상도 맛보지 않을까 이렇게 봅니다.

to function or not function. This is due to the fundamental power of this unseen aspect, as well as its ability to communicate with everything. So, as I mentioned before, when everything becomes one and functions together, that unseen aspect has incredible power to cause things to arise or to expire. Whatever confronts you, the unseen aspect can swallow it and convert it into positive energy and nutrients. You all have this incredibly helpful power within yourselves.

If people around the world raise their level of consciousness and apply this to their daily life, then everything about our lives can change, even the form of our bodies. Our future would completely change. For example, these days you're dependent upon machines when you want to use energy or to communicate with someone, but imagine a world where this could all be done by simply giving rise to a thought. This is the kind of future I'm talking about.

Don't let yourself think that this is impossible. If you think of yourself as poor, then truly, you will become poor. If you think of yourself as well-off, your life will be deeply prosperous. So don't let yourself get caught up

그렇게 할 수 없다라는 생각을 하지 마세요. 마음이 가난하면 정말 가난하게 사는 법이고 마음이 그대로 풍요로우면 정말 풍요롭게 산다 이런 거죠. 그러니 마음을 가난하고 우울하게 두지 마세요. 항상 보람 있고 생동력 있고 겸손하게 사세요. 웃는 낯으로 대하세요. 그 지혜를 무기 삼아 살림살이를 굴릴 때, 그 살림살이가 풍부해질 뿐만 아니라 여러분이 큰 대인으로서 세계적으로나 우주적으로 전체에 공헌할 수 있다는 얘깁니다. 그러면은 우리는 입으로만 진리를 말하는 게 아니라 부처님의 뜻을, 진리를 항상 그대로 실천에 옮기게 되는 것입니다. 말이 곧 진리요, 법이 된다는 얘깁니다. 두고 보십시오. 앞으로 어떻게 진행이 되는가.

과거 역사를 한번 봅시다. 찬란한 문화도 다 사람들이 발전시킨 겁니다. 그러나 그것이 지속되지 못하고 지금은 폐허가 되거나 흔적만 남아있는 그런 문화가 많습니다. 그런 걸 볼 때, 무엇이 원인이 되어 그 문화나 역사가 그렇게 풍부하게 발전이 되기도 하고, 또는 졸렬하게 되어 폐허만 남게 되는 것인지 의아한 적이 있을 겁니다. 그것은 모두 사람들의 마음이 그렇게 만든 것입니다.

in thoughts of poverty or sadness. Try to live an enthusiastic and meaningful life. Be humble. And face things with a smile.

When you put this wisdom into action in your daily life, not only will your life become happier and more prosperous, but you'll also be able to make a huge contribution to the well-being of the world and the universe. This is how we become more than people who just speculate about the reality of our world. By putting the Buddha's teachings into practice like this, your words become the truth and manifest into the world. Try this for yourself. See what happens when you put this into practice.

Take a look at history. People have given rise to great civilizations, but in many cases these couldn't continue for long, and now only exist as a few broken buildings. Looking at these cultures, you may wonder why they declined, and what led to their development. All of this was the result of how those people used their minds.

When we look at the people who played important roles in the development of a certain place, we can see that they were focused on how to improve the lives of their fellow citizens, at

과거 어느 시점에 문화를 발전시킨 사람들을 보면, 모두 잘 살자고 시작은 했는데 차츰 색(色)으로, 바깥으로 돌렸다 이겁니다. 모든 것을 자기 근본마음에 놓고 일체만법이 그 자리를 통해 자연스레 하나 되어 돌아가도록 했어야 했는데, 그렇게 하질 않고 타의로 돌리니 욕심, 원망, 증오, 싸움으로 가게 되어 결국엔 멸망할 수밖에요.

옛 성인의 말씀에 이런 게 있습니다. '남을 탓함이 없이 근본에 놓아 굴리면 내가 다시 여기 오리라.' 라고요. 여러분이 만약 일체를 내 근본마음에 놓고 돌린다면 어디 석가가 따로 있고 예수가 따로 있겠습니까? 그 찬란했던 문화를 발전시킨 사람이 따로 있겠습니까?

모두 우리 마음에 달려 있는 겁니다. 우리도 그러한 능력을 다 가지고 있는 걸요. 인간이라 하면은 벌써 내재되어 있다 이겁니다. 공급이 돼 있나 안 돼 있나 보십시오. 천안(天眼)이 있고, 천이(天耳)가 있고, 숙명(宿命)이 있고, 타심(他心)이 있고, 신족(神足)이 있습니다. 내 안에 이미 이렇게 주어져 있는데도 불구하고 그러한 내 실체를 알고 그걸 쓸 줄 모르고 거기에 따라다니는 그림자만 보고는 말려 돌아가고 있으니, 우리가 갖고 나온 그 모든 능력을 제대로 쓸 수가 없는 겁니다. 우리

least initially. But as time went by, they or their culture turned their focus outward, towards material things. This was unfortunate, because we need to always be returning everything to our foundation. Then, while functioning as one from that place, we automatically become one with everything we encounter. However, instead of doing this, they tended to compare themselves to others or to blame others, and this gives rise to desire, resentment, hatred, and eventually to fighting. It's only a matter of time before such a civilization collapses.

As an enlightened being once said, "If you entrust everything that confronts you to your fundamental mind, without blaming others, then I will return here." If you keep returning everything to your fundamental mind, how could Buddha or Jesus exist apart from you? How could you be any different from the people who developed those great cultures and civilizations?

Everything depends upon our fundamental mind. We all have such incredible potential within us. If you were born as a human being, it's already latent within you. For example, you're already endowed with the ability to see everything, to

가 그걸 마음대로 부릴 수만 있다면 국가적으로나 지구적으로나 꽃이 피게 만들어 놓을 수 있습니다. 역사나 문화나 모든 게 달라지며 우주 개발을 하는 데도 그 차원이 달라지리라고 봅니다.

그런데 내가 오신통(五神通) 얘기를 하면 사람들이 못 알아들을 수도 있어서 요새 많이 알고 있는 기계들로 그 역할을 비슷하게 둘러 얘기하기도 합니다. 예를 들면 천체망원경이라든지 무전통신기, 컴퓨터, 영사기 같은 걸로 말입니다. 단지, 자동이라는 거죠. 한생각을 내어 돌아가게 하면 대뇌로 다 통과가 되게끔 돼 있어서 자동이다 이겁니다. 그런데 그렇게 마음 낼 생각을 하지 않으니 불교가 어떻고 기독교가 어떻고 카톨릭교가 어떻고 하면서 싸우고, 내 것, 네 것 분별하면서 싸우는 겁니다. 요만한 것에서부터 큰 것까지 전부 싸워야 되는 거예요. 뭣이 내가 잘나고 네가 잘났습니까? 이 세상 일체가 다 생명 없는 게 없고, 그럼으로써 한마음 아닌 게 하나도 없이 일심(一心)으로 돌아갈 수 있는데 말예요. 그리고 사실 만물만생이 공체(共體), 공식(共食), 공용(共用)을 하고 있는데 독불장군이 어디 있다고 그렇게 야단들인지 모르겠습니다.

know others' thoughts, to know past lives, to hear everything, and to go anywhere without moving your body. Nonetheless, most people see only shadows of their true self. Because they don't see what's essential, they are easily led down useless paths. Spending all of their time and energy struggling with these, they never develop the great abilities inherent within themselves.

On the other hand, if we know how to freely use these abilities, we can cause great flowers to bloom across the nation and the world. Our culture and our future will all change, and even our ideas of space exploration will change.

Let's compare these subtle, inherent abilities to machines such as telescopes, telephones, computers, movie projectors, and so on. The five subtle abilities have these same qualities, except that they function automatically. When you return a thought to your foundation, it circulates there, and then goes to the brain where it's sent out. This is done automatically. But instead of trying to rely upon this fundamental mind, people get caught up in discriminations. They argue about Buddhism and Christianity, and fight over all kinds of ridiculous things. Those people they

'한마음 한뜻이 돼서 가라.'고 하는 이유는 그래야 우리가 살 수 있기 때문입니다. 그런데 참나를 발견하지 않는다면은 한마음으로 돌아가는지 거꾸로 돌아가는지 그걸 모릅니다. 내가 뭐 하는지도 모르면서 남은 어떻게 알 거며, 상대방을 모르는데 우주의 섭리는 어떻게 알고 대천세계의 근본은 어떻게 알 수 있겠느냐 이겁니다. 우주의 근본을 모르는 것은 내 근본을 모르는 거와 같고, 내 근본을 모르면 우주의 근본을 모르는 것과 같습니다. 그러면 한마음으로 같이 돌아가기가 힘들고, 저 행성이나 위성 또는 정보원처럼 일하는 별성의 살림이 우리네 살림살이와 별반 다르지 않다는 것도 모릅니다. 다를 게 하나도 없는데 말예요. 국방도, 정치도 다 있습니다. 없는 게 아니에요.

would look down upon are really no different than themselves. Throughout all the world, every single thing has life, so there's nothing that is not part of one mind. They are all there within one mind, and able to function as one. In fact, all things and all lives share the same body, work together as one, and freely give and receive whatever is needed. And yet people still make such a fuss, thinking that they are doing everything by themselves, or that they know better than others.

I tell people to live harmoniously, as one mind, because this is the only way forward for us. If you don't uncover your true self, you can't know whether you are acting in accord with one mind or moving in opposition to one mind. To put it another way, if you don't know what you are doing, you won't be able to understand others. If you don't understand others, how can you know the principles of the universe or the essence of the Dharma realm? If you don't know your own foundation, you can't know the foundation of the universe. If you don't know your own foundation, you won't be able to function as one mind, nor will you be able to understand life on other planets. All the same things are there —

우리가 한마음 한뜻이 돼서 조화를 이룬다면 우주 개발은 그렇게 어려운 것이 아닙니다. 우주 개발이라는 것은 다른 데다가 우리의 좋은 씨를 공급해서 다른 집에도 그 씨가 생산이 되게끔 하는 것이 개발이요, 더 나아가 생산이 잘 된다면은 바로 우리 동네 집이 된다 이 소리입니다. 혹성 하나하나, 별성 하나하나가 나 아님이 없으니 내 동네 아님이 없고 내 행동 아님이 없고, 내 모습 아닌 게 없어요. 여러분한테 내가 항상 이런 말을 하죠. 내 마음의 불씨 하나가 온누리 전체를 태워버릴 수도 있다구요. 그렇기 때문에 바로 거기에 모든 것이 갖추어져 있다는 겁니다. 자력이나 전기력, 자동력, 통신력, 이 모두가 바로 원소의 근본에 의해 돌아가고 있다는 얘깁니다.

information gathering and processing, politics, and so on. Everything on this planet is also on other planets.

If we can become one mind and function together harmoniously, then even helping with the development of the universe isn't particularly difficult. "Developing the universe" means providing good seeds of consciousness to other planets and stars, and helping those seeds to flourish. This is development. If those seeds are successful, then that place, too, becomes part of our community. Every single planet, every single star is also myself. So there's no place that isn't my community, there's no behavior that isn't my behavior, and no form of life that isn't my life. I've said this before: The spark of our fundamental mind can burn away all the karma and discriminations of the universe. This is possible because our fundamental mind is endowed with everything. Energy, the ability for everything to communicate, to function automatically, to connect — all these arise from the basic functioning of our foundation.

Some people say that life is pointless because we just get old and die, losing everything in the

간혹가다 사람들이 '변질되고 죽는 거에 허망하다.' 이러는데 내가 생각하기엔 변질되고 죽는 게 아니라 몸만 바꿀 뿐 항상 지속된다고 봅니다. 사람들은 죽는다고 말하는데 애당초에 죽는 게 어딨습니까? 이 세상에 난 것이 없는데 죽는 게 어딨습니까? 굼벵이가 지붕에서 떨어질 때는 먹은 생각이 있어서 떨어진다는 얘깁니다. '어, 굼벵이가 지붕에서 떨어지네.' 이러는 찰나에, 굼벵이는 바로 매미로 옮겨 가는 겁니다. 옮겨 가는 거지 죽어 사라지는 게 아닙니다.

지수화풍에서 미생물이 생겨 모두가 이렇게 진화돼서 살고 있습니다. 그런데 지금의 우리를 있게 한 지수화풍이 어디서 갑자기 생겨난 것도 아니고 본래의 지수화풍이 죽은 것도 아닙니다. 근본이 있기에 나온 거고 나왔기 때문에 그 자리에 있는 겁니다. 옮겨 가고 모습을 바꿔 놓을 뿐이지 지속되고 있는데 뭐가 죽고 산다는 얘깁니까? 옮겨놓고 바꿔놓는 그 사이에, 찰나찰나 옮겨 가는 고정됨이 없는 생활 속에 어찌 거기 인과응보가 붙으며 유전이 붙으며 업보가 붙으며 생사윤회가 붙겠습니까? 거기에 끄달리지 않고 자연스럽게 일렁거리면서 우리는 지금 리듬을 타고 가는 겁니다. 옮겨 놓고 지금 돌아가는 겁니다.

end. I don't see it like that. Rather, we continue on; it's just our body that we change. People talk about dying, but from the very beginning there was never any unique thing that was "born." When a larva falls from a tree to the ground, it's because it intends to become a cicada. It's not dying; it's changing its shape. It's moving from one form to another, not dying and disappearing.

Earth, water, fire, and air gave rise to microorganisms, and everything else evolved from those. These four elements that formed us didn't suddenly appear out of nothing. They arose from the foundation, and they return there. We were all born because the foundation exists, and we are here now because it exists. There is no living and dying; we're just continuously changing our shapes and moving from here to there. This is always happening every instant, with nothing remaining the same, so how could karma, genetics, causality, or the cycle of rebirth find any place to stick to? We're not actually caught by those things, we're just flowing naturally with the rhythms of the waves. We're just continuously moving from here to there.

Hmm. As I look around, some of you don't seem to understand what I'm talking about. So let

그런데 여러분들을 보니 내가 하는 이 말이 여러분한테 혼란만 주는 것 같습니다. 그만하고 결론만 얘기하자면, 여러분도 공부를 해서 부처님이 될 수 있다는 겁니다. 이 말뜻은 진정한 자유인이 될 수 있는 여건을 가졌다면 모든 것을 훌떡, 지금 현상계를 홀랑 뒤집어서 역사가 달라질 수 있는 그런 개발을 할 수 있다라는 얘깁니다. 우리가 오고 감이 없이 에너지를 공급함으로써, 필요한 양식으로써 에너지가 쓰일 수 있도록 할 수 있습니다. 모든 분야에서 발전된 역할을 할 수 있는 그런 능력이 여러분한테도 다 주어져 있다는 얘깁니다. 튼튼한 에너지원을 가지고 그 힘으로 물질을 끌어들여 목성같이 살기 힘든 행성 같은 곳에도 이익될 수 있는 에너지, 예를 들어 산소 같은 걸 만들어서 사람이나 생명이 살 수 있는 그런 기초적인 개발을 할 수 있다는 겁니다.

우리 마음이 안으로 튼튼하게 돼 있다면은 우주 개발뿐만이 아니라 폐허가 된 간이나 장 같은 데를 다시 튼튼하게 할 수 있습니다. 사람이 생동력 있게 살 수 있게 되는 겁니다. 더 나아가 우리가 **마음공부**[8]를 해서 원력이 풍부하다면 딴 동네

---

8. 마음공부: 진정한 자유인이 되기 위해 마음이 어떻게 작용하는지를 배우고, 배운 것을 실제 생활 속에서 활용하고 체험하며, 그러면서 알아가는 모든 과정을 말함.

me just jump to the conclusion: through spiritual practice, you too can become a Buddha. If you are able to become a true, free person, you can completely change everything in our world, including our future. Without ever moving your body, you could supply the energy to sustain everyone. Everyone has this ability within them. Everyone has this incredible source of energy within them. With this power, it's even possible to draw forth matter and create livable environments in harsh places like Jupiter. For example, you can lay the groundwork for sustaining life by creating more oxygen there.

If we've been consistently relying upon our fundamental mind, not only can we help with the development of the universe, we can also keep our bodies healthy. If some part of our body breaks down, such as our liver or intestines, we can help it recover. In this way, people can live with vitality.

There is a power that arises from deep and consistent practice, and if this becomes strong enough, we can even bring forth and use the energy from other stars and planets. "Far" and "near" don't exist. Although some place may be many light years away, it's all within the palm of

의 에너지도 끌어 올 수 있습니다. 멀고 가까움이 없게 됩니다. 여러분은 그것이 몇 십 광년으로 보일 테지마는 다 부처님 한 주먹 안에 있습니다, 한 주먹 안에! 모든 생명들이 자기 아님이 없으니 부처님 한 주먹 안에 있을 수밖에요. 마음이 가지 않는다면은 요 턱 밑에 있어도 천리 만리고, 마음이 한마음 한뜻으로 돌아갈 수 있다면 천리 만리에 있다 할지라도 바로 가까운 턱 밑에 있는 것입니다.

그러니 지금 이 시점에서 내가 어떻게 해야 우리를 더 발전시켜 앞으로 한국도 그렇고 세계적으로도 원료가 부족치 않게 할 수 있는지, 진정으로 나라를 위하고 지구를 위하는 길이 뭔지 알아야 합니다. 원료를 부족치 않게 할 수 있는 그런 힘도 우리에게 있다는 거를 알아야 합니다. 마음공부를 하다 보면 어떻게 해서 그렇게 되는 지도 알게 되고 그렇게 실천으로 옮길 수도 있습니다.

Buddha's hand. It's all right here, because there is nothing that's not also yourself. If we try to reach out to something without going through our fundamental mind, then even though it's right in front of us, it may as well be a thousand miles away. However, if through our fundamental mind we become one with something, then even though it's a thousand or a million miles away, it's as if it were right next to us.

Therefore, at this critical moment, you have to know how to take care of others, as well as our planet. What's the path forward that will allow us to help develop our nation and the world? How can we ensure that there will be enough energy and resources? You need to know that we have within us the power to answer all of these questions. The ability to provide sufficient energy and other resources is within us. As you practice relying upon your fundamental mind, how to take care of all these things will become clear to you.

In the old days, you had to use your body to protect the nation and to do things like politics or commerce. Now, all of those things can be done without moving your body. You can become one with other people, and other people can become

예전에는 몸뚱이가 다니며 나라도 지키고 정치도 하고 무역도 했지만 지금은 앉아서 할 수도 있어요. 그걸 화신력(化身力)이라고 한다면은 우리가 그 사람이 되는 겁니다. 마음은 내놓을래야 내놓을 것도 없고 빛깔도 없고 줄 것도 없습니다. 그렇기 때문에 내가 상대방이 될 수 있고 상대방이 내가 될 수 있는 거죠. 예를 들어, 국방부에서 일을 한다면 내가 국방부장관이 되어서 나라가 이익되는 대로 이끌고 갈 수 있지 않겠느냐는 얘깁니다. 정치인이라면 정치인대로 사람들의 마음을 소상히 알아서 그 사람이 돼주면 될 거 아닙니까?

이거는 지금 몸뚱이를 보고, 색을 보고, 말을 하는 걸 들어서 그런 위대한 인간을 뽑으라는 게 아닙니다. 그런 시대는 벌써 지났습니다. 우리도 앉아서 그 사람 마음을 볼 줄 알아야 합니다. 앉아서도 그 사람 마음과 하나가 되어 같이 움죽거려 줘야 합니다.

one with you, because mind has no form and nothing to grasp. In ancient times, this ability was called the power of manifestation. For example, in order to lead the country in a positive direction, I can also become one with the defense minister. If I become one with a politician, then it's as if I'm lending them my wisdom and spiritual ability so that they can do good for the country.

Similarly, the time has passed when we can choose people for such positions based upon their appearance, their background, or how well they give speeches. Instead, we have to be able to know their minds. We have to know how, through our fundamental mind, to become one with people and function together with them.

A person involved in politics needs to be aware of the unseen aspect that underlies politics. Could this be called something like a god? No, not really. It's not this and it's not that. Yet, it's there in the middle of everything. It's this fundamental mind that can embrace and take care of anything in the entire universe. It can bring in and send out anything through the sense organs, and if you've awakened to this mind, you can become one with politicians and act through them. There's

정치를 하는 사람은 정치를 하되 정치를 하게끔 해주는 무언가가 있다는 걸 알아야 합니다. 이것도 아니고 저것도 아닌 그 가운데, 한 점의 마음이 우주를 덮고 들고 굴릴 수 있는 그런 마음이, 바로 오관을 굴릴 수 있는 그런 마음이 여러분에게 있다면 바로 여러분이 정치인과 하나가 되어 직접 하는 겁니다. 나 아님이 없고 내 자리 아님이 없고 내 아픔 아님이 없고 내 말 아님이 없는데 어찌 그것이 안되겠습니까? 역사를 바꾸고 올바른 개발을 하고 문화가 발전이 되고 꽃을 피울 수 있고 조화를 이루게 할 수 있다는 거죠.

만약에 좀먹는 벌레가 식물에도 있고 동물에도 있고 또 여러 생물에 다 있다면, 그 벌레들을 한데 합쳐서 바로 내가 하나가 되어 진화시켜 보십시오. 그러면 연쇄적으로 하나도 버릴 게 없게 되니까요. 그렇게 하지 않으면 버려야 될 것들이 너무 많이 있거든요.

nothing that's not myself — there's no pain that's not my pain, no circumstances that aren't my circumstances, no words that aren't my words. So how could you not become one with someone? Because of this, we can change the direction of our society, we can ensure upright development, and we can ensure that our culture blossoms and is harmonious.

For example, there are insects and parasites that harm plants and animals, right? Through your fundamental mind, you can gather their consciousnesses all together and help them evolve. If you can do this, then you can use this method to embrace everything. There's no one and nothing that you need to throw away. Otherwise, you'll have to chase after so many things, trying to get rid of them one by one. There are just too many things to deal with them like that.

If you would improve the level you're living at, take all of those things that you would throw away or exclude, and entrust them all to the great furnace within you. There, they will all be melted down, and will come back out as something good. You'll never be able to raise your level by manipulating the material world, or through scholarly knowledge or cleverness. Take all the

이것이 지금 중세계의 지구 안에 있는 현실인데 그 살림살이에서 2차원, 3차원, 4차원, 5차원, 6차원, 7차원까지 올리려면은 그 좀먹는 것들을 다 한데 용광로에 넣어서 좋은 물건으로 생산하는 그런 작업이 필요하다 이겁니다. 이거는 물질을 보고 하는 거 가지고는 도저히, 학식이나 지식을 가지고는 도저히 할 수 없는 겁니다. 여러분이 갖고 있는 학식이나 지식을, 분야가 어떠한 것이든 몰락 한꺼번에 넣어서 거기에서 참자기가 살아나야 됩니다.

그건 무슨 소리냐 하면 여러분이 지금 살고 계신 그 자체가 그대로 참선(參禪)이고 행선(行禪)이니, 그 안에서 몰락 놓고 생활해야 된다는 얘깁니다. 어디 가서, 바깥에서, 무슨 형상을 찾고, 위대한 이름을 찾고, 허공에서 연구하려고 골치를 썩히지 마십시오.

오직 '만법의 근원이 어디로부터 나오나? 참다운 내가 있기 때문에 모든 게 나오는 것이 아닌가? 또 참다운 내가 있기 때문에 모든 거를 오관을 통해서 들이고 있지 않는가? 주인공, 당신이 억겁을 통해서 나를 끌고 다녔는데 내가 당신 은혜를 모르겠는가? 나는 당신의 은혜를 알 터인즉 당신은 나를 올바르게 이끌고 가거라.'라고 하십시오. 그러면 알고자 하는 걸 알 수 있습니다.

things you know, and all that you've learned, and dump them entirely into this furnace; then, your true self will come alive, and your level will change.

What I'm saying is that your life right now, just as it is, should be meditation, and meditation in action. So live while taking everything that comes up in your life and completely letting go of it to this furnace. Don't give yourself a headache by searching around outside of yourself, chasing after famous practitioners, looking for holy relics to worship, or searching for "special" places to practice.

What's the origin of everything? It all arises from our true self. This true self brings in and sends out absolutely everything through our sense organs. It's the one that does everything, the one that has been leading us and taking care of us for untold billions of years. Now that you know what it does, trust that it will take care of you. Living like this is the essence of meditation, and if you keep doing this, that which you're seeking will be revealed.

If you have to meditate by sitting down and crossing your legs, then as soon as you stand up,

몸으로만 좌선을 하고 앉았다가 일어나면 벌써 선(禪)은 끊어지게 돼 있습니다, 참선이 끊어져요. 그런데 그걸 어떻게 선이라고 하겠습니까? 자기 수련은 할 수 있을지언정, 몸을 단련을 해서 조복은 할 수 있을지언정 어떻게 그것으로 이 크나큰 뜻을 알 수 있겠습니까? 은산철벽을 어떻게 뚫을 수 있겠습니까?

그러니 하나도 떨어트리지 말고 가십시오. 들고 나는데 티끌 하나도 붙을 자리가 없다는 그 도리를 아셔야 합니다. 걸리지 마셔야 합니다. 그렇다고 도둑질을 하면서 '그 자리에서 시키는 거니까 괜찮아.' 한다면 이건 천만의 말씀입니다. 인간으로 태어났다면 기본적인 상식과 교양과 질서를 아시리라고 믿습니다. 그러니까 그런 상식 밖의 말에 대해서는 덧붙이지 않아도 될 거라고 믿습니다.

your meditation is over. How could that truly be called Seon (Zen)? Sitting meditation and other kinds of physical training may be useful sometimes, and if you train your body hard enough, or sit long enough, your thoughts will calm down and you'll feel a sense of peace. But that's not enough. That can never lead you to the great meaning. Those kinds of practices can never help you penetrate the silver mountains and iron walls.

Go forward entrusting everything to your foundation, without missing a single thing. Know that although everything enters and leaves you, there's no place for even the tiniest piece of gunk to stick to. Don't let anything trip you up, including what you hear from inside. If you think it's acceptable to steal others' property because it seemed like your true self said so, well, that's just nonsense. Anyone born as a human being has at least a basic sense of good judgment, fairness, and propriety. So it's not necessary for me to say more about things like this, things that are so far outside the realm of common sense.

People who are serious about spiritual practice need to throw everything into this

공부하는 여러분은 기독교니 불교니 카톨릭교니 이슬람교니 이런 모든 것을 자기 마음의 용광로에다 다 넣어 버리고 녹여라 이겁니다. 그렇게 녹이면 거기에서 생산이 되는 것은 아마 이 세상에 보배가 될 것입니다.

여러분이 이름을 따로 지어 붙인 거지 진리가 어디 따로 있습니까? 우리가 타고 있는 이 배는 그냥 희희낙락 놀고 구경하기 위해 탄 배가 아닙니다. 지금 이 순간에 어디로 달리고 있는 줄은 아십니까? 여러분은 이 배가 어디로 달리는지도 모르고 속수무책으로 가고 있습니다. 허허바다 어디에 있는지, 어디까지 왔는지도 몰라요. 우리는 지금 바깥을 내다볼 여지가 없습니다. 그건 왜냐? 별성이나 지구가 돌아가는 대로 똑같이 따라가기 때문입니다. 그러기 때문에 우리는 여기가 어딘지 어디까지 왔는지 그걸 모릅니다. 그런데 그 안에 살면서 뭘 그렇게 많이 안다고 내것, 네것 가르고 헐뜯으며 무슨 말이 그렇게 많습니까?

furnace that is our fundamental mind, including all ideas of Buddhism, Christianity, Islam, and so forth. Melt everything down there; then what arises again from that will be a treasure of this world.

Names and labels are made by dividing things, but is there anything that could exist outside of the truth? No. The ship you are now on isn't some pleasure cruise. You don't even know where it's going. You're just helplessly along for the ride. On this vast ocean, you don't even know where you are, let alone where you've come from. Just following along with things, it never even occurs to you to try to look outside the boat. Not knowing where the boat has come from or where it's going, how could you be so certain in your opinions, insisting that you know so much, criticizing others, and getting into all kinds of arguments?

Let's compare the Earth to your body. The Earth also has organs that function like the stomach, liver, kidneys, and intestines. In order for each part to live, they have to cooperate. They have to work together. But what happens if they are always arguing with each other? If they start laying

이 지구가 내 몸이라면 내 몸 속에 대장, 소장, 간, 위장, 직장, 이자, 콩팥이니 뭐니 이런 것들이 이 안에서 같이 살림을 하고 있는데, 같이 도와야 살 수 있는데 왜 그렇게 말이 많습니까, 도대체. 이 부분은 내 것이고 이 부분은 네 것이고, 이렇게 갈라놓으면 이 몸이 죽어요! 지구가 없어진단 말입니다! 한 부분이 나빠지면 벌써 그곳은 폐허가 되지만 한마음 한뜻으로 조화가 된다면 폐허가 될 수 없습니다. 그러니 역사가 달라지죠. 조그마한 나 하나 끌고 다닐 줄 모르면서, 나 하나 조화를 이룰 줄 모르면서 어떻게 내 가정, 사회, 국가, 세계, 우주를 밝게 보고 밝게 듣고 밝게 응용할 수 있겠습니까?

불교가 어떤 겁니까? 밥이나 놓고 빌면서 귀신 단지처럼 내 고귀한 생명을 어디다가 맡기고 살게 하는 그런 존재입니까? 그런 게 종교입니까? 그런 것이 불교입니까? 그리고 여러분 중에도 부적해다가 맨날 베개 밑에 넣는가 하면 주머니에 달고 다니고 이러는데, 그러지 마세요. 자기가 이 세상에 나와서 그냥 갈 수 없는 고귀한 보배인 줄을 모르

claim to different areas, and building walls around "mine" and "yours," your body will die! The Earth, too, will die if something like this happens. If one place goes bad, soon everything that depends upon that area will collapse. Yet if minds become one and harmonious, then that collapse can be prevented. And then the direction of our society changes as well. Listen! When you don't even know how to take care of yourself, when you argue with others and close yourself off to them, how could you be able to clearly see, to clearly hear, and to wisely respond to even your family, to say nothing of society, the world, or the universe?

What is Buddhism? Is it something that teaches you to entrust your precious life to superstitions? Could such a thing be called Buddhism? I know there are some people here who've bought talismans, and keep them in their pillows or walk around with them in their pockets. Stop doing this. You were born to be a precious one — someone who would do something wonderful in this world. Will you waste your time here with useless pieces of paper? Why would you entrust your precious life to those? Relying on things outside yourself like talismans can

고 하찮은 그런 종이 짝에 쓴 거를 가지고 그걸 신주단지 모시듯 하면서 자신의 고귀한 생명을 거기다가 맡겨요? 그렇게 맡기는 그런 게 종교가 아닙니다. 여러분은 똑바로 알고 똑바로 행하셔야 될 것입니다.

우리의 이 고귀한 마음이 그대로 생동력 있게 숨쉬고 있고 움죽거리고 있습니다. 이것이 바로 부처님입니다. 한생각을 내딛으면 **법신**(法身)[9]이 되는 거고, 한생각을 또 내딛으면 화신이 되는 겁니다. 여러분은 부처가 따로 있고, 신장(神將)이 따로 있고, 의사가 따로 있고, 판사가 따로 있는 줄 알지만 여러분 한생각에 그런 것들이 다 될 수 있는 겁니다. 그리고 지금 보이는 것만 있는 줄 아십니까? 여러분 몸 속에 수십억 생명이 여러분의 부하로서 우물거리고 있습니다. 여러분을 모시고 말입니다. 공장장들이요, 회장을 모시고 다닙니다. 여러분 생각해 보세요. 얼마나 성스럽고 얼마나 기쁘고 좋습니까?

---

9. 법신(法身): 부처의 몸이 다양한 중생들을 구제하기 위하여 여러 모습으로 나타난다고 하는데, 응신(應身), 보신(報身)(혹은 화신(化身))과 함께 삼신(三身) 중의 하나. 진리를 체득한 깨달음의 본질이 현실에서 작용하게 되는 것으로, 대행큰스님은 근본자리에서 올라오는 마음이 발현되는 것이 법신이라고도 설명하심.

hardly be a true religion. You need to understand what's truly going on — you need to understand your fundamental mind — and you need to put that understanding into action.

This most precious mind of ours is what allows us to breathe in and out, to move, and to live with vitality. It is Buddha itself. If we entrust a thought to this precious, fundamental mind of ours, it comes back out as the Dharma. If we apply this to the things in our life, it manifests into the world. Usually, when you see Buddhas, Dharma-protecting spirits, doctors, judges, and so on, you're probably seeing these and automatically thinking of them as apart from yourself. However, by entrusting a single thought to your foundation, you can become all of these. Do you only believe in what you can see with your eyes? Really? Inside your body, right now, there are billions of lives that are working unseen on your behalf. They're all serving you. You, the CEO. Do you have any idea how sacred and delightful you are?

The servants that are taking care of your body have even put up defenses around every single cell, protecting each of them from outside intruders. Why are you turning your back on

여러분을 모시고 다니는 부하들이 세포 하나하나마다 이렇게 망을 치고선 어디에서 뭐가 들어올까봐 막아주고 이러는데, 자기를 위하는 자기의 생명들을 어찌 그렇게 무시하고 남한테다 의존하고 이럽니까? 몸이 아파 어쩔 수 없이 의사한테 의존을 해야 한다 하더라도 의사와 내가 둘이 아니어야 됩니다. 그 마음도 둘이 아니어야 하고 또한 내 속에 병이 난 그 부분에 있는 생명들도 나하고 둘이 아니어야 됩니다. 그래야 폐허가 되지 않고 병이 생겼다가도 잘 아물어질 수가 있고, 또는 한마음으로 조화가 돼서 병이 씻은 듯이 나을 수가 있는 겁니다.

병뿐만 아니라 살아나가는 일이 모두 그렇습니다. 바깥일도 그렇고 집안일도 그렇고 여러 가지로 다 그렇습니다. 시를 쓰는 시인이라 할지라도 살아있는 시를 쓰는 그런 시인이 되지 못하고 죽은 시를 쓰는 그러한 분들이 돼서는 안되죠. 글을 쓰든 춤을 추든 온통 야단을 하더라도 그게 살아있는 것이 돼야지 죽은 것이 돼서는 아무 의미가 없습니다.

these servants who are ceaselessly protecting you, and instead trying to rely upon others? Why aren't you trying to rely upon your foundation? When you're hurt or sick, it may be necessary to go see a doctor, but become one with that doctor! Your mind has to become one with that doctor, as well as with the beings within you who are ill. Then your body won't be damaged, and even if you have a disease, it won't cause big problems. If you can become one mind and function harmoniously with the lives within you, the disease may even completely disappear.

This applies to every aspect of our lives, at home and in society, as well as illnesses. For example, even if you're writing poetry, you should create living poems that have the power to touch people. Don't be someone who comes up with clever, dead poems. No matter whether you're writing, dancing, or whatever you do, it must be something alive! If it's dead, it's pointless, because it can't deeply connect with people.

Please listen carefully, even though I can't speak eloquently. If I were thinking about trying to come up with sophisticated or clever ways of expressing myself, my words would be useless.

나는 말도 조리 있게 할 줄 모릅니다마는 여러분이 조리 있게 들어주십시오. 내가 세련되게 말을 하려고 이렇게 저렇게 생각을 하게 되면 진실된 말이 나오질 않습니다. 그걸 이해해 주세요.

나는 이 중요한 한마디 한마디를 그냥 한데 떨어트리게 할 수는 없습니다. 막말로 죽은 뒤에 천당 가고 극락 가려고 그러는 게 아닙니다. 천만에요. 이 다음에 죽어서 잘 되고 어떻고 하는 거 신경 안 씁니다. 내가 여러분에게 올바른 한마디를 해주기 위해 나를 불사르고 타면서 피가 흐른 게 몇 바가지나 되는 줄 아십니까? 칼이 오든 가시덩쿨이 오든 자갈밭이 오든, 현실에 내가 체험하고 넘어서야 돼요! 내 목숨 하나 내놓는다면 그뿐인 걸 뭐가 그렇게 두렵고 어렵습니까? 칠십 평생을 살다 죽든 어린애 때 죽든 한 번 죽는 겁니다.

They would lack the deep connection with the truth that living words have. They would have no true power to help others. Please understand this principle.

I'm not telling you about these things out of some hope for something for myself, either in this life or next. Even though the energy it costs me to give you deeply true guidance feels like it could be measured in cups of my blood, I don't care. Do you know why? Because we have to face whatever confronts us without fear. Whether you are facing swords, thorns, or fields full of rocks, don't flinch from any of it. Do your best to go forward taking it all as something to practice with. What are you afraid of? Whether you die in your youth or in old age, you'll still have to die once. If you can let go of the fear of dying, there's nothing you cannot do. Nothing can scare you.

And yet, even dying isn't something extraordinary; it is only changing shapes. I can't begin to describe how many times you've died and changed your shape. Even in this very life, you're continuously dying and changing, dying and changing, bit by bit, until, all at once, you change a lot. This is how we're living our lives.

그런데 앞서도 얘기 했지만 죽는 게 별게 아니라 모습이 바뀌는 게 죽는 겁니다. 과거생부터 지금까지 몸 바뀐 건 말할 것도 없고 현생에서도 매번 변화되고 죽고 또 죽고, 죽고 또 죽고 이렇게 모습을 조금씩 바꾸다가 나중엔 홀딱 다 바꿔버리는 이러한 이치에서 우리는 살고 있는 겁니다. 그 와중에도 바뀌지 않는 건 내 주인공, 내 근본뿐입니다.

살다 보면 그 무엇보다도 돈을 제일로 중하게 여기는 분들을 만나기도 합니다. 그래서 그런 분들에게 이 돈은 지금 자기가 관리하는 거지 영원히 자기가 가지고 가는 게 아니라고 해도 받아들이지를 못해요. 영원히 지속적으로 가지고 가면서 살림살이하는 게 있다 해도 그걸 못 알아듣는 겁니다. 또 어떤 사람들은 현생의 재물이란 당분간 내가 가지고 있는 걸로 알고, 내가 당분간 쓰는 걸로 알라고 하니까 허망하다고 아무렇게나 쓰는 사람도 있고, 아깝다고 꽉 쥐고 있는 사람도 있고, 별의별 분이 참 많아요. 그러나 돈은 버는 것보다도 쓰는 게 더 어려운 일이라는 걸 아셔야 됩니다. 그러니 많이 벌고 싶으면 제대로 쓰는 것부터 배우세요.

The only thing in the middle of all of this that doesn't change is your Juingong, your foundation.

You've probably met people who think that nothing is more important than money. I try to explain to them that money isn't even something we own; we only manage it for a short while. But they just don't want to hear this. When I tell them that there is something eternal within us that is always working on our behalf, they don't have any idea what I'm talking about. When some people hear that money and property are ours for only a short while, they respond by clinging ever more tightly. Still others respond by just wasting their money, spending it like water. Sigh. People have so many different ways and levels of thinking! You should know, however, that spending money wisely is actually harder than earning it. If you want to have a lot of money, you'd better start by learning how to spend it wisely.

People have gone to jail for even stealing a loaf of bread, haven't they? Could a piece of bread really be worth all that hardship? Yet that decision only took an instant. Just one thought, one decision can completely change our lives. Long ago, Jesus told those who wished to taste his kingdom to come forward, leaving behind

겨우 빵 하나를 훔치다가 징역까지 살기도 합니다. 그깟 빵 하나가 얼마나 된다고 말이에요. 그런데 한 순간의 선택이 그런 우스운 일도 만들어냅니다. 옛날에 예수님이 내 떡 하나 얻어먹으려면 네 재산을 다 가져오라고 그랬습니다. 부처님께서도 이 공부를 하려면은 권속과 재물을 다 떼어놓고 오라고 했습니다. 그리고 또 그러한 마음을 떼어놓고 오라고 했습니다.

세상에 마음 하나 잘 내는 게 얼마나 중요한지 아십니까? 뭐이 그렇게 영원히 자기 것이라고 욕심을 냅니까? 사실 알고 보면 내 것 네 것 없이 참 여여(如如)[10]하게 그렇게 좋을 수가 없는데 말이에요. 모든 게 자기 주인 것이지 내 것이 아니라고 생각을 해야죠. 이 육신조차도 내 것이 아니니 말입니다. 제 성품에 의해서 지금도 움죽거리고 있으니 그 성품 주인에게 다 맡겨버리세요.

---

10. 여여(如如): 만물만생이 평등하고 차별 없이 어디에도 머물지 않고 끊임없이 흘러 돌아가고 있는 그대로의 모습. 일체가 고정됨이 없이 돌아가는 진실의 모습을 말하며, 이러한 진리의 흐름에 부합하는 삶을 살아가는 것을 여여한 삶이라 함.

all of their possessions. The Buddha, too, said that those who wished to undertake this practice should set aside their attachments to families and possessions.

Do you realize how important raising a good thought can be? Why do you have so much energy wrapped up in objects of desire, thinking they'll be yours forever? How can I even express how wonderful it is when there is no "mine" and "yours"? When everything is complete just as it is? You have to understand that nothing is yours; it all belongs to that which is fundamentally doing everything. Even this body isn't yours. It's functioning because of your true nature, so you have to entrust everything about it to your true nature.

Long ago, *Kyongho*[10] Sunim met some boys gathering firewood in the mountains, and bet them that they couldn't hit him. If they could,

---

10. Kyongho Sunim (鏡虛惺牛, 1846-1912) was the greatest Seon master of his era, and is responsible for much of the current vitality of Korean Buddhism. He had five great disciples, one of whom, Hanam Sunim, was Daehaeng Kun Sunim's teacher. Over fifty percent of the Buddhist monks and nuns in Korea can trace their lineage directly back to him.

예전에 경허(鏡虛)스님[11]이 나무꾼더러 돈을 줄 테니 때리라고 했답니다. 그래서 때렸더니 "나 경허는 맞지 않았다." 이러더랍니다. 그러니 나뭇꾼이 안 때리거든요. 때리면 돈 준다고 그랬는데 맞지 않았다니까 돈 안 줄까 봐 안 때리거든요. 그래서 "내 선돈 줄께 때려라." 그랬답니다.

이게 그냥 웃기는 이야기로 들리겠지만 그렇지 않습니다. 제대로 배우려면 돈 주고 배워야 한다는 말 아시죠? 이 공부하는 데 얼마나 많은 시련과 얼마나 많은 공덕(功德)[12]이 쌓여야 되는지 여러분은 짐작도 할 수 없을 겁니다. 다만 여기서 지금 가르치는 것만이라도 속속들이 빨리 깨우치고 실천해 가는 그런 과정을 거치면 좋겠습니다.

오늘은 이걸로써 마치겠습니다.

---

11. 경허선사(鏡虛, 1846-1912): 조선말기, 억불숭유로 바람 앞 촛불 같던 때, 한국불교의 선맥을 되살린 선지식이며 대강백이셨다. 대행스님은 경허스님의 5대 제자 중 한 분이신 한암스님의 제자스님.

12. 공덕(功德): 이 책에서의 의미는 다른 사람이나 대상을 나와 둘로 보지 않고 '내가 했다.'라는 생각을 하지 않으며 조건 없이 도와주는 상태, 혹은 그렇게 함으로써 나오는 결과를 뜻함. '함이 없이 하는 것' 즉, '내가 이러이러한 일을 했다.' 라는 생각을 놓아버리고 해야 공덕이 되는 것이다. 아무런 조건 없이 하는 행(行)이라야만 만물만생에게 이익이 될 수 있음.

he'd give them a few coins. So they swung and hit him, but he shook his head, saying they'd missed. The boys began to cry and stopped trying because it seemed like he was cheating them. So Kyongho Sunim held out some coins, "Okay. Here's an advance payment. Keep trying to hit me." This may seem like just a silly story, but it is very much not.

Have you ever heard the expression that if you truly want to learn something, you have to pay for it? You cannot imagine the hardships you've gone through, nor how much *virtue and merit*[11] you've accumulated to reach this point where you are ready and the circumstances are right for you to learn about the practice of relying upon your fundamental mind. So it is my deepest wish that you will take what I've said here today and diligently work at putting it into practice, until you understand this to your very core.

Thank you. Let's stop here for today.

---

11. Virtue and merit (公德): Here this term refers to the results of helping people or beings unconditionally and non-dually, without any thought of self or other. It becomes virtue and merit when you "do without doing," that is, doing something without the thought that "I did such and such." Because it is done unconditionally, all beings benefit from it.

한마음출판사의 마음을 밝혀주는 도서

- A Thousand Hands of Compassion
  만가지 꽃이 피고 만가지 열매 익어
  : 대행큰스님의 뜻으로 푼 천수경 (한글/영어)
  [2010 iF Communication Design Award 수상]
- Wake Up And Laugh (영어)
- No River To Cross, No Raft To Find (영어)
- It's Hard To Say (영어) (절판)
- My Heart Is A Golden Buddha (영어)
- Touching The Earth (영어) (2014 new)
- Moonlight In A Thousand Rivers (한글/영어) (2014 new)
- 생활 속의 참선수행 (시리즈) (한글/영어)
  1. 죽어야 나를 보리라
     (To Discover Your True Self, "I" Must Die)
  2. 함이 없이 하는 도리
     (Walking Without A Trace)
  3. 맡겨놓고 지켜봐라
     (Let Go And Observe)
  4. 마음은 보이지 않는 행복의 창고
     (Mind, Treasure House Of Happiness)
  5. 일체를 용광로에 넣어라
     (The Furnace Within Yourself)
  6. 온 우주를 살리는 마음의 불씨
     (The Spark That Can Save The Universe, 2014 new edition)
  7. 한마음의 위력
     (The Infinite Power Of One Mind, 2014 new)
  8. 일체를 움직이는 그 자리
     (In The Heart Of A Moment, 2014 new)

9. 한마음 한뜻이 되어
   (One With The Universe, 2014 new)
10. 지구 보존
   (Protecting The Earth, 2014 new)

- 내 마음은 금부처 (한글)

- 건널 강이 어디 있으랴 (한글)

- El Camino Interior (스페인어)

- Vida De La Maestra Seon Daehaeng (스페인어)

- Enseñanzas De La Maestra Daehaeng (스페인어)

- Práctica Del Seon En La Vida Diaria (Colección) (스페인어/영어)
   1. Una Semilla Inherente Alimenta El Universo
      (The Spark That Can Save The Universe)

- Si Te Lo Propones, No Hay Imposibles (스페인어)

- 人生不是苦海 (번체자 중국어) (2014 new edition)

- 无河可渡 (간체자 중국어) (2014 new)

- 我心是金佛 (간체자 중국어) (2014 new)

외국출판사에서 출판된 한마음도서

- Wake Up And Laugh
  Wisdom Publications, 미국

- No River To Cross
  (*No River To Cross, No Raft To Find* 영어판)
  Wisdom Publications, 미국

- Wie Fließendes Wasser
  (*My Heart Is A Golden Buddha* 독일어판)
  Goldmann Arkana-Random House, 독일

- Ningún Río Que Cruzar
  (*No River To Cross* 스페인어판)
  Kailas Editorial, S.L., 스페인

- Umarmt Von Mitgefühl
  ('만가지 꽃이 피고 만가지 열매 익어':
  대행큰스님의 뜻으로 푼 천수경 독일어판)
  Diederichs-Random House, 독일

- 我心是金佛
  (*My Heart Is A Golden Buddha* 번체자 중국어판)
  橡樹林文化出版, 대만

- Vertraue Und Lass Alles Los
  (*No River To Cross* 독일어판)
  Goldmann Arkana-Random House, 독일

- Wache Auf Und Lache
  (*Wake Up And Laugh* 독일어판)
  Theseus, 독일

- Дзэн И Просветление
  (*No River To Cross* 러시아어판)
  Amrita-Rus, 러시아

- Sup Cacing Tanah
  (*My Heart Is A Golden Buddha* 인도네시아어판)
  PT Gramedia, 인도네시아

- Không có sông nào để vượt qua
  (*No River To Cross* 베트남어판)
  Phuong Nam Books, 베트남 (2014 출판예정)

- *No River To Cross*
  (*No River To Cross* 아랍어판, 제목미상)
  Sphinx Publishing, 이집트 (2015 출판예정)

Books by Daehaeng Kun Sunim
-available through Hanmaum Publications

- A Thousand Hands of Compassion (bilingual, Korean/English) [received **2010 iF communication design Award**]
- Wake Up And Laugh (English)
- No River To Cross, No Raft To Find (English)
- My Heart Is A Golden Buddha (English)
- Touching The Earth (English) (Forthcoming 2014)
- Moonlight In A Thousand Rivers (bilingual, Korean/English) (Forthcoming 2014)
- *Practice in Daily Life* (Series) (bilingual, Korean/English)
  1. To Discover Your True Self, "I" Must Die
  2. Walking Without A Trace
  3. Let Go And Observe
  4. Mind, Treasure House Of Happiness
  5. The Furnace Within Yourself
  6. The Spark That Can Save The Universe
  7. The Infinite Power Of One Mind
  8. In The Heart Of A Moment
  9. One With The Universe (Forthcoming 2014)
  10. Protecting The Earth (Forthcoming 2014)
- 건널 강이 어디 있으랴 (Korean)
- 내 마음은 금부처 (Korean)
- El Camino Interior (Spanish)
- Vida De La Maestra Seon Daehaeng (Spanish)
- Enseñanzas De La Maestra Daehaeng (Spanish)

- Práctica Del Seon En La Vida Diaria (Series) (bilingual, Spanish/English)
  1. Una Semilla Inherente Alimenta El Universo
- Si Te Lo Propones, No Hay Imposibles (Spanish)
- 人生不是苦海 (Traditional Chinese)
- 无河可渡 (Simplified Chinese)
- 我心是金佛 (Simplified Chinese) (Forthcoming 2014)

-Books available through other Publishers

- No River To Cross
  Wisdom Publications, U.S.A.

- Wake Up And Laugh
  Wisdom Publications, U.S.A.

- Wie Fließendes Wasser
  German edition of *My Heart Is A Golden Buddha*
  Goldmann Arkana-Random House, Germany

- Vertraue Und Lass Alles Los
  German edition of *No River To Cross*
  Goldmann Arkana-Random House, Germany

- Umarmt Von Mitgefühl
  German edition of *A Thousand Hands Of Compassion*
  Diederichs-Random House, Germany

- Wache Auf Und Lache
  German edition of *Wake Up And Laugh*
  Theseus, Germany

- Ningún Río Que Cruzar
  Spanish edition of *No River To Cross*
  Kailas Editorial, S.L., Spain

- 我心是金佛
  Traditional Chinese edition of *My Heart Is A Golden Buddha*
  Oak Tree Publishing Co., Taiwan

- Дзэн И Просветление
  Russian edition of *No River To Cross*
  Amrita-Rus, Russia

- Sup Cacing Tanah
  Indonesian edition of *My Heart Is A Golden Buddha*
  PT Gramedia, Indonesia

- Không có sông nào để vượt qua
  Vietnam edition of *No River To Cross*
  Phuong Nam Books, Vietnam, Forthcoming 2014

- *No River To Cross* (*title to be determined*)
  Arabic edition of *No River To Cross*
  Sphinx Publishing, Egypt, Forthcoming 2015

한마음선원본원

경기도 안양시 만안구 석수동 101-62
Tel : 82-31-470-3100   Fax : 82-31-470-3116
홈페이지 : http://www.hanmaum.org
이메일 : jongmuso@hanmaum.org

국내지원

강릉지원 (우)210-940 강원도 강릉시 포남2동 1304
 TEL:(033) 651-3003   FAX:(033) 652-0281

공주지원 (우)314-870 충청남도 공주시 사곡면 신영3리 152-3
 TEL:(041) 852-9100   FAX:(041) 852-9105

광명선원 (우)369-900 충청북도 음성군 금왕읍 대금로 1402번지
 TEL:(043) 877-5000   FAX:(043) 877-2900

광주지원 (우)502-270 광주광역시 서구 치평동 201-5
 TEL:(062) 373-8801   FAX:(062) 373-0174

대구지원 (우)706-838 대구광역시 수성구 수성로 41길 76번지
 TEL:(053) 767-3100   FAX:(053) 765-1600

목포지원 (우)530-490 전라남도 목포시 상동 952-19
 TEL:(061) 284-1771   FAX:(061) 284-1770

문경지원 (우)745-823 경상북도 문경시 산양면 반곡리 449번지
 TEL:(054) 555-8871   FAX:(054) 556-1989

부산지원 (우)606-080 부산광역시 영도구 동삼1동 522–1번지
 TEL:(051) 403-7077   FAX:(051) 403-1077

울산지원 (우)683-500 울산광역시 북구 천곡동 927-7
 TEL:(052) 295-2335   FAX:(052) 295-2336

제주지원 (우)690-140 제주도 제주시 영평동 1500
TEL:(064) 727-3100 FAX:(064) 727-0302

중부경남 (우)621-802 경상남도 김해시 진영읍 하계로 35번지
TEL:(055) 345-9900 FAX:(055) 346-2179

진주지원 (우)660-941 경상남도 진주시 미천면 오방로 528–40번지
TEL:(055) 746-8163 FAX:(055) 746-7825

청주지원 (우)360-814 충청북도 청주시 상당구 우암동 295-7
TEL:(043) 259-5599 FAX:(043) 255-5599

통영지원 (우)650-110 경상남도 통영시 도천동 113-3
TEL:(055) 643-0643 FAX:(055) 643-0642

포항지원 (우)791-220 경상북도 포항시 북구 우현동 13-1
TEL:(054) 232-3163 FAX:(054) 241-3503

Anyang Headquarters of Hanmaum Seonwon
(430-040) 101-62 Seoksu-dong, Manan-gu, Anyang-si
Gyeonggi-do, Republic of Korea
Tel: (82-31) 470-3175 / Fax: (82-31) 470-3209
www.hanmaum.org/eng
onemind@hanmaum.org

Overseas Branches of Hanmaum Seonwon
ARGENTINA
Buenos Aires
Miró 1575, CABA, C1406CVE, Rep. Argentina
Tel: (54-11) 4921-9286 / Fax: (54-11) 4921-9286
www.hanmaum.org.ar

Tucumán
Av. Aconquija 5250, El Corte, Yerba Buena,
Tucumán, T4107CHN, Rep. Argentina
Tel: (54-381) 425-1400
www.hanmaumtuc.org

BRASIL
Sao Paulo
R. Newton Prado 540, Bom Retiro
Sao Paulo, C.P 01127-000, Brasil
Tel: (55-11) 3337-5291
www.hanmaumbr.org

CANADA
Toronto
20 Mobile Dr., North York, Ontario M4A 1H9, Canada
Tel: (1-416) 750-7943 / Fax: (1-416) 981-7815
www.hanmaumcanada.org

GERMANY
Kaarst
Broicherdorf Str. 102, 41564 Kaarst, Germany
Tel: (49-2131) 969551 / Fax: (49-2131) 969552
www.hanmaum-zen.de

THAILAND
Bangkok
86-1 soi 4 Ekkamai Sukhumvit 63
Bangkok, Thailand
Tel: 070-8258-2391 / (66-2) 391-0091
home.hanmaum.org/bangkok

USA
Chicago
7852 N. Lincoln Ave., Skokie, IL 60077, USA
Tel: (1-847) 674-0811
www.buddhapia.com/hmu/chi/

Los Angeles
1905 S. Victoria Ave., L.A., CA 90016, USA
Tel: (1-323) 766-1316
home.hanmaum.org/la

New York
144-39, 32 Ave., Flushing, NY 11354, USA
Tel: (1-718) 460-2019, 070-7883-5239
Fax: (1-718) 939-3974
www.juingong.org

Washington D.C.
7807 Trammel Rd., Annandale, VA 22003, USA
Tel: (1-703) 560-5166 / Fax: (1-703) 560-5566
http://home.hanmaum.org/wa

본 서적과 관련하여 문의 사항이 있으신 분은
아래의 연락처를 이용해 주시기 바랍니다.

한마음국제문화원/한마음출판사

경기도 안양시 만안구 석수동 101-60
전화: (82-31) 470-3175
팩스: (82-31) 470-3209
e-mail: onemind@hanmaum.org

If you would like more information about these books or
would like to order copies of them,
please call or write to:

**Hanmaum International Culture Institute
Hanmaum Publications**

101-60, Seoksu-dong, Manan-gu, Anyang-si
Gyeonggi-do, 430-040, Republic of Korea
Tel: (82-31) 470-3175
Fax: (82-31) 470-3209
e-mail: onemind@hanmaum.org